Building with the Community

Engineering projects to meet the needs of both men and women

Brian Reed & Ian Smout

Water, Engineering and Development Centre
Loughborough University
2005

WEDC

People-centred solutions
for sustainable development
since 1971

© WEDC, Loughborough University, 2005

Reed, B. J. and Smout, I. K. (2005)
Building with the Community:
Engineering projects to meet the needs of both men and women

A reference copy of this publication is also available online from:
http://www.lboro.ac.uk/wedc/

ISBN 13 Paperback: 9781843800811
ISBN Library Ebook: 9781788532785
Book DOI: http://dx.doi.org/10.3362/9781788532785

A catalogue record for this book is available from the British Library.

This document is an output from a project funded by the UK
Department for International Development (DFID)
for the benefit of low-income countries.
The views expressed are not necessarily those of DFID.

This edition is reprinted and distributed by Practical Action Publishing.
Since 1974, Practical Action Publishing has published and disseminated books and information in
support of international development work throughout the world. Practical Action Publishing trades
only in support of its parent charity objectives and any profits are covenanted back to Practical Action
(Charity Reg. No. 247257, Group VAT Registration No. 880 9924 76).

Designed and produced at WEDC
by Glenda McMahon and Rod Shaw

Acknowledgements

This introduction was produced by a project team consisting of Sue Coates, Marie Fry, Sarah Parry-Jones and Brian Reed, led by Ian Smout. The research and development of this booklet and the associated guidelines and training material was assisted by the following partner organisations:

• Mvula Trust (South Africa)
• CSIR (South Africa)
• UNICEF (India)

... together with other valuable contributions including by staff from UNICEF (Nigeria), WaterAid (Zambia) and Médecins sans Frontières.

The funding for the project was provided by the UK Department for International Development as part of their engineering Knowledge and Research programme (KAR). This booklet is one of the outputs from project R7129.

Brian Reed

Contents

Introduction

Engineers and technicians working on development projects are becoming more aware of the need for the participation of local people, and that women, in particular, should be involved closely at all stages of the project cycle. This booklet sets out why engineers should involve both men and women in infrastructure projects and why women's participation has a special emphasis. It introduces ways in which engineers and technicians can ensure their projects focus on the needs of men and women.

Although many people working on development projects will be aware of these issues, others may not be. As well as providing an introduction for engineers and technicians who have not covered some of the social issues before, this booklet is also useful for managers who do understand the issues but are seeking ways to tackle these, or for those who wish to explain the problems and solutions to their colleagues.

The aims of engineering projects

Ask engineers what the main objective of their project is and you may get a reply such as "build a water supply system" or "construct an irrigation canal". Ask them why and you may get an answer such as "to provide drinking water" or "to enable crops to be grown".

Ask policy-makers why they want a water supply, irrigation canal or new road and the reply might be about health or economic growth. Some governments and organisations may be a bit more specific and say they are reducing poverty, as expressed in the Millennium Development Goals.

Poverty reduction is not just an economic issue. People can improve their lives by using the various resources that they have, such as:

- financial resources (e.g. access to credit, savings schemes – ranging from micro-credit to investing in livestock);
- human resources (e.g. skills, knowledge, being healthy);
- natural resources (e.g. land, water, fisheries, biodiversity);
- social resources (e.g. relationships, membership of groups); and
- physical resources (e.g. infrastructure, roads, water supplies).

By looking at all these aspects of people's lives, it may be possible to improve their access to one or more of these resources and provide them with opportunities to make their lives better. Provision of physical resources may not increase opportunity by itself. The structures of government and the private sector, or the way in which the organisations work, may be a limiting factor.

Infrastructure and people's livelihoods

Engineers do play a part in improving people's lives. Providing infrastructure and setting up organisations to manage public services can have a dramatic impact on all aspects of their lives. The most obvious contribution is to the physical environment, providing roads or drainage, but these have both positive and negative effects. Laying a water pipeline is not a neutral action, but can provide benefits of clean, safe water or costs of diverting water away from a former use. The impacts can be physical, economic, social or environmental.

• Roads can improve communication, enhancing social links or access to markets, but can increase the spread of diseases (Figure 1).

• Water supply and sanitation can improve health, but needs to be maintained and paid for. The costs to people should be less than the benefits they perceive.

• Irrigation can improve access to natural resources and increase crop production, but can favour those who can afford other inputs, such as fertilizer.

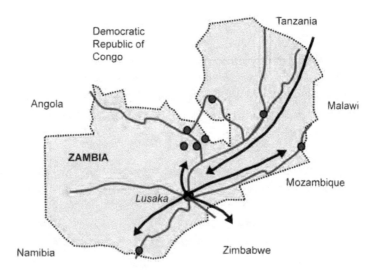

Figure 1. The spread of HIV/AIDS along roads in Zambia

Source: From *The effects of HIV/AIDS on agricultural production systems in Zambia,* Adaptive Research Planning Team, Ministry of Agriculture, Food and Fisheries, for the FAO, 1993

- Planned drainage can protect existing valuable aquatic ecosystems and prevent pollution of the environment; unplanned drainage can make the situation worse.

- Employing people to build the infrastructure can support the local economy. The training provided to manage infrastructure will increase human resources, even in areas not related to the original project. Meeting on committees or around a handpump can create a focus for a community, supporting social networks.

The different resources that are available to people are inter-related. Lack of access to one resource may reduce the value of another resource. Thus, natural resources may be enhanced by increasing a physical resource such as irrigation or transport to markets. Providing human resources, such as skills and encouragement may increase financial resources. Similarly, physical resources, such as water supplies, may only be fully used if other resources are enhanced, such as bringing local skills and knowledge into the planning and provision process. People may decide not to use a water supply if it has not been designed with the needs of their situation in mind.

Understanding communities

If engineering projects are going to address society's needs, engineers will have to have some understanding of society. Often sociologists or social scientists have this task of analysing and assessing the community's needs, but they are not engineers. If the benefits of the project are to be maximized, sociologists will have to understand what engineers can offer the community and engineers will need to know something about the community. The two professions need to work together with *each other and the community.*

One of the types of analysis social scientists carry out is looking at the different groups in society (e.g. rich, poor, men, women, race, class, caste), although some think that everybody is individual and you cannot categorize people into groups. Modern theories now suggest that you assess people as individuals *and* as members of the various groups that they may belong to. Whatever method of analysing society is used, you can be sure that it will not be a simple homogeneous group. An engineering parallel would be geology, where you can class rocks into broad groups, but each piece has its own individual strengths, composition and characteristics. You use terms like 'sedimentary' or 'gneiss' to describe a rock in general terms, but you would still want to carry out a site survey before starting design.

Social scientists look not only at different groups in society, but also at how they interact. Understanding the power relations within a community is important, especially where these relationships exclude people from decision-making and voicing their opinion.

Different groups in society will use infrastructure in different ways. In some societies men may use water for watering livestock, whilst women use it for irrigating vegetable crops. The rich may travel on roads for long distances, with few stops on their journey, whilst the poor use the same road for more frequent, but shorter journeys, walking and stopping to meet neighbours.

The following Venn diagram shows a simple model of society. This could be for any society, with the proportion of rich and poor changing.

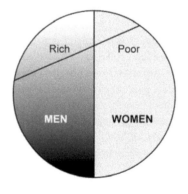

Figure 2. An idealised Venn diagram of a community

There are two facts that can be seen from this diagram. Firstly there are many more poor people than rich people. This proportion increases for less developed countries. Secondly there are more poor women than poor men. If a project was being planned to benefit the whole of society, the planners should be aware that the demands of one group of people do not necessarily reflect the demands of other groups. People are members of many groups at the same time, so a rich man from a village does not necessary reflect the wishes of all the villagers although they all live in the same area.

This does have an impact on planning projects. If the goal is to reduce poverty, and the means to do this is to improve people's health or to increase their access to economic activities by providing infrastructure, then the infrastructure must support the overall goal and meet the needs of the poor. The needs of poor men and poor women may be different however. Women not only form the greatest proportion of the poor, but also on average are poorer than the men. If a peasant male farmer is poor, then a peasant female farmer is likely to be poorer, economically, socially and in access to other resources.

There are more women in poverty than men. Women that are widowed, abandoned wives and women with husbands working away from home have fewer opportunities open to them than men do. Women have less access to education, property and finance. They may have to carry out domestic jobs and care for children as well as try to earn an income. Married women may not have access to all of their husband's income, although they may be responsible for the household expenditure. This may be a problem if water, food or fuel has to be paid for. Husbands may have provided cash payment for a water connection (capital expenditure), but it may be the woman who is responsible for the on-going bills (operational expenditure). Figure 3 shows who normally collects water in Bhutan.

Involving women

Women not only form a greater proportion of the poor, and therefore should feature prominently in a poverty reduction programme, but also meeting their needs is normally a better investment than looking solely at projects that meet men's needs. Women are often responsible for household management, so improvements in their income are more likely to be spent on the household, improving the health and economic well-being of the whole family. Teaching good hygiene practice is more likely to get used in the home and passed onto children and neighbours if women and men are specifically targeted than if only men were involved.

Women also are more concerned with some types of infrastructure. Often water collection is the responsibility of women and so is the care of sick members of the family. Developments such as water supplies or improved health through sanitation and solid waste management will have more of an impact on women's

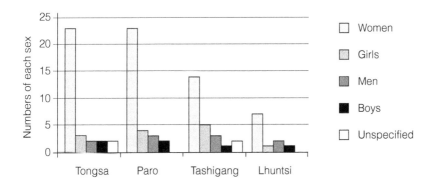

Figure 3. Main water collectors – Bhutan

Source: Marie Fry, from data collected in a PRA exercise in Bhutan

lives than on men in the same community. Women cook, so are more concerned with the supply of food, cooking fuel and the pollution from stoves than men.

These *domestic* tasks can be supported by the provision of infrastructure – water supplies, sanitation, irrigation and transport for food security and domestic energy for cooking and heating. The work of engineers directly supports these tasks. Figure 4 shows how women have domestic duties in *addition* to productive work.

Concentrating solely on women though will ignore other groups in the community, such as men or the poor. Consulting with women may result in rich, more confident women being involved and this may not

help poor women who may have different priorities. If men are excluded from the benefits of a project, they may not be so supportive. For this reason analysis has to be not only pro-poor, but also look at the needs of men and women separately and then assess them together. It is no good improving a water intake for domestic water supply (targeting women), if there is pollution upstream from (male) industrial or agricultural activities. A longer-term issue is to address *why* there are these inequalities between social groups.

It has to be remembered that women already have a heavy work load – not formal, paid work, but domestic work, small-scale agriculture and child care. Asking women to contribute to project

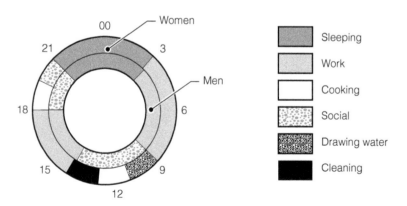

Figure 4. A clock chart recording a day's activities

Source: Example from *Planning for construction and rehabilitation* PCU/CMMU/WASHE, Zambia

planning, construction and maintenance may give them even more work. This has to be addressed for each situation, checking people are happy to take on this extra burden in return for the benefits that the project should produce. Engineers need to be able to negotiate with the whole community, at times and places when it is convenient for each group, and take these factors into account when designing a project.

Engineers are good at balancing competing demands such as efficiency, safety, durability and cost of structures. The needs of the whole community are another important factor that should be included in the design process. Figure 5 shows how the hydraulic design of a water supply system may work, but the location of tap stands has disadvantaged vulnerable people.

Increasing project efficiency

It is now a well-established fact that involving women in certain engineering projects improves the chances of the project succeeding and meeting its targets. Many projects have failed because they did not address the demands of the people they were meant to serve. Examples include pumps being

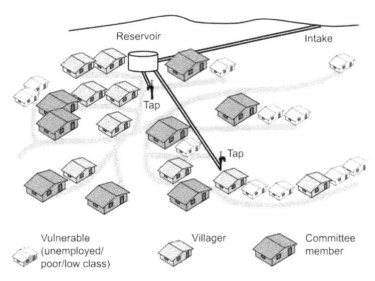

Figure 5. Location of water taps in a village

Source: Deepa Joshi, Map of Chuni village, India

Box 1. Gender jargon

Engineers use specific terms to describe ideas – consider the engineering senses of *stress* and *strain*. These have clear meaning to engineers, but a non-engineer may not think stress is force per unit area.

Sociologists have their own set of technical terms. One term is *gender*. This does not mean somebody's sex (which is a biological term), but society's *responses* to somebody's sex; how a person's sex influences their social, legal and economic status. Thus the fact that women in one community do not usually ride bicycles, but men do, is not determined by the physical differences between the groups, but what society expects of each group. In a neighbouring society women cycle, as the expectation of the community is different.

Observations from Small Towns Water Supply and Sanitation Project team, between people living in the Buganda and Busoga areas in Uganda.

Box 2. Men and women's uses of water

In some societies men are responsible for mainstream agriculture. Irrigation of these crops or livestock can be shown to be financially beneficial in cash terms. Women on the other hand may be responsible for subsistence agriculture, such as smallholdings for the family's food. The produce from these "gardens" may not have a cash value or be traded in the market, but it is vital for the local economy and the welfare of the family.

If there is a drought, competition for water may mean that the few men who farm cash crops and have better access to decision-makers may have priority over the numerous women farmers for water rights, with obvious impacts on the family.

The water sources may also be different; men may be using conventional water sources such as wells or canals. Women may be competing for these water sources, but may also use less recognised water sources, such as rivers for washing clothes in, or harvesting water from roofs for household use.

sited for political reasons (e.g. outside an influential person's house), rather than where the main collectors of water (often women) really wanted it. The project does not only have to be built with the users in mind, but should be able to be operated by the community. Many projects now train women as hand pump caretakers as they have an interest in keeping the pump working. In a study of 121 projects, Deepa Narayan (World Bank, 1995) found that effective projects tended to be participatory, although participation did not always manage to include women.

However, the technical gains in efficiency by involving men and women in projects can only work if they can contribute effectively. If a woman has been trained as a pump caretaker but is not allowed to take part in making decisions about the pump, then she will not be able to maintain it effectively. The process of social transformation is called *empowerment* by social scientists. Thus the practical engineering (e.g. location of the pump) and the technical skills (e.g. maintenance training) have to be supported by social action if people who are normally excluded from society are going to be able to participate in the project. The socially excluded (e.g. the poor or women) need to gain both self-esteem, so they can explain their needs, and also public esteem, so their views are asked for *and* respected.

People however are not just economic units, to be used to ensure a job is

---

**Box 3.
Example of empowerment**

Women in one area of India protested that the water department had not repaired their pump. Working with an NGO, the water department trained teams of women to maintain their own pumps and supported their work in the district. The handpumps were repaired and now there are very few out of order. The NGO also helped them in other areas, such as education.

Jacob Pfohl Mainstreaming Gender in WES UNICEF 1998.

---

completed on time, on budget and serves the majority of the population. People are also individuals and should be treated with respect. This is an issue of the rights of men and women as well as the efficiency and effectiveness of the project.

Why are men and women not involved?
Empowerment may help people feel they can voice their opinions, but there are many barriers that prevent people, such as poor women, from being involved in engineering projects. These can be either:

• within the community or

• external to the community.

These barriers may be due to a variety of factors, such as:

- *Cultural issues*. Women may be prevented or deterred from speaking in public or meeting with men without a relative present.

- *Legal issues*. Women may not be allowed to hold public office or own land – despite that fact that there are more female farmers worldwide than male farmers.

- *Institutional issues*. Girls may not be offered schooling, water for domestic use may not be seen as a priority or disposal of solid waste (which is a household issue) is not funded but a new hospital (which is a municipal issue) is.

The external barriers reinforce these problems. Engineers need to be aware that their actions may add to the exclusion of certain groups of people. Local and external engineers may have their own cultural assumptions that influence their decision-making and they should be aware of this.

Various policies have been promoted to try to overcome these problems. Design specifications may ignore the poor. Consider a road design based on cars and lorries, this gives less priority to the needs of pedestrians.

Box 4. Cultural assumptions

One engineer from the north of an African country was disturbed to see women digging on a small construction site. Where he came from women did not do that sort of work. In the south-west however, women dig the fields and build houses and so informal construction work was not inappropriate.

Patrick Nyeko, Uganda

Policy and practice

National water or sanitation policies often only cover technical issues. Departments, agencies and organisations have developed policies in an attempt to redress some of the imbalances in the impact that projects have on different people[1]:

- Developmental policies are designed to enhance the abilities of people in socially excluded groups (e.g. financial assistance for education, management assistance for small businesses)

- Preferential policies take a more direct path, giving disadvantaged groups more opportunities. This can provide rapid change but may lead to the selection of less qualified people and raise doubts about the merits of all those who are selected.

[1] Based on: World Development Report 2000/2001, The World Bank

Policies to enhance the involvement of men and women need to have some tangible outputs, just as a water supply may have physical, financial and health outcomes.

Social projects that specifically target vulnerable or excluded groups in society may seem to be the obvious route to promote more sustainable livelihoods for these men and women. This however still treats the "problem" separately and this can marginalize the action. Infrastructure projects may assume that the gender issue can be ignored as it is being covered elsewhere. This may lead to increased empowerment of the socially excluded groups, but they may miss out on the benefits the infrastructure project was meant to bring. Leaving them out of the project may also mean the project does not meet its aims, wasting time, money and engineer's efforts. If the only people who are motivated to maintain for example, a sewerage system, are women – because they have to clean up when it blocks, then they should be given the skills to carry out the work and the system should be designed with them in mind.

Box 5. Dublin Principles

At the 1992 International Conference on Water and the Environment in Dublin, four guiding principles were adopted. Principle 3 states:

Women play a central part in the provision, management and safeguarding of water.

The role of the engineer

One method of overcoming the treatment of social exclusion as a special issue is to integrate social policies with other development projects – such as the provision of infrastructure. This is sometimes called *mainstreaming*. This shifts the responsibility of involving men and women from specialists to the whole project team. Within the team there may be social scientists to carry out some tasks, but every member of the team needs to be involved. On some projects, there may be no social scientist and the engineer has to undertake this role. Engineers have a broad education and often work in areas that are not part of their core skills – such as contract law or hydrogeology.

There are various ways an engineer can implement polices of social inclusion.

• Being aware of the issues and accepting they are real. Personal attitudes are important. How people think influences how they act.

• Engineers can ensure there is good communication with all members of the team. In return, engineers need to be able to explain the different technical and management options that are available throughout the project. The implications of alternative options should be discussed. They should do this with the minimum of engineering jargon and make the issues relevant to their audience.

• Engineers need to listen to people working in other subject areas, so they can understand and accept the issues they are dealing with.

• In their own work, engineers can also make a difference. Ensuring that infrastructure is designed with those people who are building or operating it in mind. Well walls should not be so high that women cannot use them; tap stands should be of a design acceptable to the users; toilets should be designed to suit men, women and children's different requirements. Discussing with all sectors of the community may lead to the best solution.

• Respect the opinions of women and consult the users on a wide range of issues. Employ women – where possible, on the project. Figure 6 shows a group exercise where men and women discussed the design of a latrine slab such as the position of footrests.

Fully integrating gender issues into infrastructure projects can maximise the impact of a development project, improving both the engineering and the social aims.

How can engineers involve men and women?

To carry out these policies, however, engineers need to gain an awareness

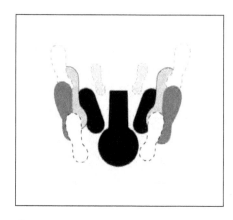

Figure 6. Engineers design pit latrines – but who uses them?

of the issues involved and understand some of the methods that may be used. There are many publications and training materials that cover this subject. Many of them have been written for a social scientist audience. However there are some resources prepared for engineers and managers.Consider a simple engineering problem, such as the design of a parapet for a dug well; how high should it be?

Too high and people will not be able to lean over and draw water; too low and young children may fall in and animals or stormwater may cause pollution. Deciding what size to select could be a matter of measuring the height of the population and basing the design on this information.

It may not be clear who actually collects the water, and a design based on the average adult may not be suitable for girls. A design for men may not be suitable for women who may not have the strength to haul buckets in the same manner as men. Only through talking to the various sectors of the community can the designer discover who the users will be and what their requirements are.

Participatory methods encourage local people to discuss project issues with professional staff. Established methods not only provide information, but encourage the involvement of all members of society. Some methods concentrate on socio-economic factors or promote empowerment, but they can be adapted to meet engineer's needs.

Figure 8. Discuss with the users what height the well wall should be

Practising what you preach

Engineering organisations can also respond to the diverse nature of society. An assessment of the social mix of a government department or consultancy may be led by policy or justice issues. However, there are also very pragmatic reasons for having inclusive work practices. Having a workforce that reflects the wider community will help the organisation respond to the community's needs. Female engineers, with appropriate training, do have greater opportunities for talking to women's groups than a male colleague would. Having a transparent, participative management system will give greater legitimacy to these principles if they are promoted externally to clients and communities.

Figure 7. A child reaches over the wall of a well. Does one size fit all?

Box 6. DFID objectives

The UK Department for
International Development plans to:

*"Secure greater livelihood security,
access to productive assets and
economic opportunities for women
as well as men."*

They plan to do this by:

• Improving access for women
  to affordable energy, water,
  sanitation and transport services

• Adhering to core labour
  standards

• Developing family friendly
  employment practices

• Improving information flows

• Ensure local planning and
  access to natural resources is
  gender aware

Engineers and managers of
infrastructure projects are key
people in implementing these
actions to meet the objective.

*Poverty elimination and the
empowerment of women,
DFID, 2000*

Box 7. Whose pit latrine design?

In drawing up a specification, what
are the important details?

Builders want...
• Pit and superstructure
  dimensions
• Material type, quantities and
  availability
• Location of latrine
• Labour required (skills and time)
• Number of users
• Type and cost
• Time scale for building and what
  season

A woman with a baby wants...
• Located somewhere safe
• Located near the house
• No smell and little or no fly
  attraction
• Easy to clean
• Have water available for washing
• Affordable
• Big door
• A light

The community leaders want...
• Long lasting
• Affordable
• Simple to construct
• Safe to use
• Acceptable by the community

*WaterAid, Zambia and
students at WEDC*

In terms of employment, restricting your pool of employees does not make good business sense. The Institution of Civil Engineers in the UK is promoting "Respect for People[2]" in order to recruit and retain talented people and maximise productivity for the industry. Ways to enhance diversity in the engineering workforce are similar to those measures that can be adopted with community projects:

• Short-term, practical measures. These include physical issues, such as making sure that the office has appropriate toilets and is in an accessible location. Practical human resource actions include considering flexible hours, maternity and paternity leave, fieldwork arrangements and pay levels. These may remove some of the barriers that prevent people from joining, contributing to and remaining with an institution.

• Longer-term, strategic action. Just addressing the practical issues about people's physical and social requirements will not by itself create equality of opportunity. One indicator of an organisation that does have a diverse workforce is to look at the proportion of women at each level of management and in each department. This is only a simple measure, as

having one or two women in positions of power may only be a token presence with little influence. The proportion of women should be compared to a benchmark, but what that level should be is not clear. There are two methods to include the excluded in the workplace.

• One method is to employ, develop and promote staff to higher levels of management; this may involve enabling people to gain qualifications and experience and monitoring recruitment and employment practices.

• The other method is to devolve power, so decisions are made at a lower level. This may be achieved by flattening the management structure or by forming smaller, more intimate project groups.

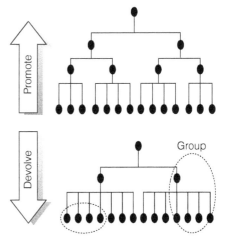

Figure 9. Promote or devolve

---

[2] An initiative promoting diversity in the workplace, welfare on site, health and safety, career development, lifelong learning and off-site working environments.

Key points

• Engineering projects normally provide a service. The product (road, water supply, irrigation canal) is not the objective, but a means of improving people's lives, economically, socially and physically.

• Society is not uniform; there are rich and poor, men and women, the influential and the excluded.

• Different groups in society use infrastructure in different ways. Truck drivers and pedestrians both use roads, but in different ways.

• Infrastructure projects should meet the needs of all users if they are going to maximise the return on the investment.

• Widespread indicators of groups of people often excluded from decision-making are their wealth and sex. Poor women have less influence than rich men.

• Women are often responsible for domestic work. This is unpaid and has a low status, but is important for the well being of the family.

• Water for drinking, cooking, washing and growing food is often the responsibility of women.

• Practical steps can be taken to alter engineering designs to suit the needs of women.

• Engineers can enhance the status of women and other excluded groups by the way they manage projects.

• Engineers' organisations can also exclude people; taking practical steps and altering management structure can open up opportunities for all.

Other outputs include:

Infrastructure for All: Meeting the needs of both men and women in development projects – a practical guide for engineers, technicians and project managers. (WEDC 2006)

Developing Engineers and Technicians. (WEDC 2006)

Case studies of relevant projects.

For further details see: http://www.Lboro.ac.uk/wedc/

Printed in the USA
CPSIA information can be obtained
at www.ICGtesting.com
JSHW072029140824
68134JS00044B/3839